THINGS TO MAKE AND DO

ALL ABOUT LUNAR NEW YEAR

KEVIN TSANG

ILLUSTRATED BY LINH NGUYEN

SCHOLASTIC

FOR MY MUM AND SISTER, WHO MADE THIS BOOK POSSIBLE – KT

DEDICATED TO MY PARENTS AND SISTER FOR GIVING ME A WONDERFUL CHILDHOOD, AND TO MY HUSBAND FOR ALWAYS BELIEVING IN THE ARTIST IN ME – LN

Published in the UK by Scholastic, 2022
1 London Bridge, London, SE1 9BA
Scholastic Ireland, 89E Lagan Road, Dublin Industrial Estate,
Glasnevin, Dublin, D11 HP5F

SCHOLASTIC and associated logos are trademarks
and/or registered trademarks of Scholastic Inc.

Text © Kevin Tsang, 2022
Illustrations by Linh Nguyen © Scholastic, 2022

ISBN 978 07023 1523 7

A CIP catalogue record for this book is available from the British Library.

Printed by C&C Offset Printing Co., Ltd in China
Paper made from wood grown in sustainable forests
and other controlled sources.

1 3 5 7 9 10 8 6 4 2

www.scholastic.co.uk

This copy of

ALL ABOUT LUNAR NEW YEAR:
THINGS TO MAKE AND DO

belongs to:

_____

_____

Learn all about the Lunar New Year festivals
celebrated by billions of people all over the world
every year, and the events that lead up to them!

This book is packed full of crafts and delicious recipes
for you to make and share with friends and family.

Don't forget: you can find definitions of the words
in **bold** in the glossary at the back of the book.

LUNAR NEW YEAR
AROUND THE WORLD

Lunar New Year is celebrated all over the world. It marks the beginning of a new year based on the **lunisolar calendar** and it is the most important annual celebration for many East Asian and Southeast Asian countries.

In China, the Lunar New Year is known as **Chūn Jié**, in Vietnam it is called **Tết Nguyên Đán** and in Korea it is known as **Seollal**. People in Taiwan, Singapore, Indonesia, Malaysia, Myanmar, Thailand, Cambodia and the Philippines also celebrate Lunar New Year.

The festival falls on a different day every year – it is usually between 21 January and 20 February. The celebrations start on New Year's Eve, and can last for up to sixteen days!

In China, billions of trips are made each year for the Lunar New Year – so many trips that it is considered the largest annual human **migration** on the planet! More than 2 billion people celebrate Lunar New Year – that is around 20 per cent of the world's population.

WHAT IS THE LUNISOLAR CALENDAR?

Most people use the **Gregorian calendar**. It is a solar calendar, which means it uses the **Sun** to keep track of time. A year is divided by twelve months and has 365 days. **Earth** takes 365.25 days to orbit the Sun, so we add a leap day to February every four years to match the calendar to Earth's **orbit** of the Sun.

The lunisolar calendar is based on the lunar (**Moon**) and solar cycles. A new Moon marks the start of a new month and each new year begins on the second (or sometimes third) new Moon after the winter **solstice**. A solstice occurs twice a year when one of the Earth's poles reaches its furthest

distance from the Sun – depending on which **hemisphere** you are in, it will be the shortest day of sunlight of the year, and the longest day in the other hemisphere! The lunisolar calendar has leap months – some years have thirteen months – so that the years align with the Gregorian (solar) calendar.

The lunisolar calendar dates as far back as 3,000 BCE. In the past, people used to track the lunar cycle (phases of the Moon) as it helped them keep track of time. The solar calendar was used to track the movement of the Sun and keep track of the changing seasons. Lunar New Year is celebrated at the beginning of each new year based on the lunisolar calendar.

THE
CHINESE ZODIAC

Originating in China, the Chinese **Zodiac** has been adapted and is used in many East Asian and Southeast Asian countries. There are twelve animals in the zodiac and each have their own unique characteristics.

Find your birth year in the grid on the next page – your zodiac animal will be at the top of that column. Then look up your characteristics in the list below.

Rat: quick-witted, charming and ambitious

Ox: dependable, patient and determined

Tiger: brave, confident and competitive

Rabbit: friendly, compassionate and sincere

Dragon: kind, fearless and lively

Snake: clever, graceful and captivating

Horse: energetic, independent and outgoing

Goat: empathetic, nurturing and artistic

Monkey: playful, mischievous and curious

Rooster: outgoing, adventurous and resourceful

Dog: helpful, honest and loyal

Pig: loving, intelligent and diligent

RAT	OX	TIGER	RABBIT	DRAGON	SNAKE	HORSE	GOAT	MONKEY	ROOSTER	DOG	PIG
1900	1901	1902	1903	1904	1905	1906	1907	1908	1909	1910	1911
1912	1913	1914	1915	1916	1917	1918	1919	1920	1921	1922	1923
1924	1925	1926	1927	1928	1929	1930	1931	1932	1933	1934	1935
1936	1937	1938	1939	1940	1941	1942	1943	1944	1945	1946	1947
1948	1949	1950	1951	1952	1953	1954	1955	1956	1957	1958	1959
1960	1961	1962	1963	1964	1965	1966	1967	1968	1969	1970	1971
1972	1973	1974	1975	1976	1977	1978	1979	1980	1981	1982	1983
1984	1985	1986	1987	1988	1989	1990	1991	1992	1993	1994	1995
1996	1997	1998	1999	2000	2001	2002	2003	2004	2005	2006	2007
2008	2009	2010	2011	2012	2013	2014	2015	2016	2017	2018	2019
2020	2021	2022	2023	2024	2025	2026	2027	2028	2029	2030	2031
2032	2033	2034	2035	2036	2037	2038	2039	2040	2041	2042	2043

THE GREAT RACE

Legend has it that the Jade Emperor wanted a way to keep track of time so he decided to make a Zodiac. He held a Great Race to decide which animals to include and what their order in the Zodiac should be.

The details of this legend vary, but in one well-known version thirteen animals raced across a large river: an ox, a dog, a tiger, a rabbit, a cat, a pig, a dragon, a snake, a rat, a horse, a rooster, a monkey and a goat (depending on how the Chinese Zodiac is translated, the goat can also be a sheep or a ram. The Vietnamese Zodiac has a cat instead of a rabbit). The order they finished the race determined their order in the Zodiac.

FIRST (RAT) AND SECOND PLACE (OX)

Before the race started, the rat and the cat knew that the other animals were faster and stronger, and to finish the race first, they would need help. They convinced the ox, who was strong, to carry them on its back.

The ox raced ahead of the other animals! But the rat was cunning and wanted to be the one to win the race. First, it pushed the cat into the river. Then, just before the ox finished the race, the rat jumped off its back and raced ahead, finishing first.

THIRD (TIGER), FOURTH (RABBIT) AND FIFTH (DRAGON) PLACE

The tiger did well in the race and finished third. If it weren't for the trouble the tiger had with the river's current, it might have finished first.

The rabbit was very fast, hopping from stone to stone in the river, but it slipped and fell in. Luckily, it grabbed a floating log and rode the log to a fourth-place finish.

How did a powerful dragon finish fifth you might ask? Well, the dragon was as kind as it was fierce, and it stopped to help a village in need. It also saw the rabbit floating the wrong way down the river and blew a puff of air to get it back on course. By the time the dragon finished the race, it was in fifth place.

SIXTH (SNAKE) AND SEVENTH (HORSE) PLACE

The horse wasn't far behind the dragon. But, before it crossed the finish line, the snake, who had coiled itself around one of the horse's legs, sprang free and took sixth place. The startled horse finished right after in seventh place.

EIGHTH (GOAT), NINTH (MONKEY) AND TENTH (ROOSTER) PLACE

Stranded on the shore, the goat, the monkey and the rooster decided to work together to finish the race. They built a raft and successfully navigated the river. They finished in eighth, ninth and tenth place.

ELEVENTH PLACE (DOG)

While the dog was a very strong swimmer and could have finished earlier, it couldn't resist the urge to play in the water and finished eleventh.

TWELFTH PLACE (PIG)

The pig stopped to eat some food and fell asleep. But it woke up in time to complete the race, finishing in twelfth place and completing the Zodiac.

WHAT ABOUT THE CAT?

After the rat pushed the cat into the river, the cat never finished the race and didn't make it into the Chinese Zodiac. Legend has it that this is why cats and rats don't get along to this day and why cats don't like water!

THE KOREAN ZODIAC

The Korean Zodiac consists of the same twelve animals as the Chinese Zodiac and they also appear in the same order. However, the legend of how these animals earned their spot in the Zodiac is different. It is said that long ago, Buddha invited all the animals in the world to visit him, but only twelve showed up! Buddha rewarded these twelve animals by including them in the Korean Zodiac in the order that they arrived.

THE LEGEND OF NIAN

Legend has it that in ancient China there was a monster called Nian. Nian had horns and sharp teeth and lived at the bottom of the sea. On New Year's Eve, Nian would rise from the depths and wreak havoc on villages.

Year after year, Nian would destroy crops and attack the people of the village until it was discovered that Nian had a weakness. Nian was frightened by the colour red, firelight and loud noises.

The next year, the villagers wore red clothes, made lots of noise by banging on drums and made light by burning bamboo – they scared Nian away! He never came back. Now people do this every year to celebrate Nian's defeat.

THE LEGEND OF
THE PEACH TREE

Long ago there was a peach tree on the east side of the Soc Son Mountain in Vietnam. Two deities, Trà and Uất Luỹ, lived in this tree and protected the local villagers from demons and evil spirits. At the end of each year, Trà and Uất Luỹ returned to heaven for a meeting with its ruler, the Jade Emperor.

To keep the villagers safe while they were away, Trà and Uất Luỹ told them to break a branch off a flowering peach tree and put it in their home. The evil spirits were so afraid of these two deities that even the sight of a peach tree would frighten them. This is why many people who celebrate Tết have an ornamental tree or branch on display in their home.

Many who celebrate Tết also have a kumquat tree (a symbol of good luck and prosperity) in their homes. It is said that the more fruitful the tree, the luckier your family. It also symbolizes the family as the fruit: flowers, buds and new green leaves represent the grandparents, children and grandchildren. These trees are carefully chosen and displayed in the home.

TRADITIONS

SWEEPING AND KEEPING

Prior to the new year, it is customary for homes to be swept to sweep out the bad luck. The broom and dustpan are hidden away before New Year's Day so that the good luck that arrived with the new year isn't swept away!

CELEBRATIONS

As lots of countries and cultures celebrate Lunar New Year, the holiday is rich with tradition. The following pages offer a few examples of the traditions and beliefs that are celebrated during this time. There are many examples as even regions within the same country have different customs.

Many of the traditions are highly symbolic, from the colours you wear, to the food you eat, and the activities you should and shouldn't do. It is a time to get together with family; to wish good luck, good fortune and good health to others; and to ward away evil spirits and bad luck for the coming year.

To give a sense of some of the Lunar New Year customs, here's a few traditional beliefs about what those celebrating should and shouldn't do on New Year's Day or during the holiday.

DO

- Reunite with family
- Prepare and share New Year foods, such as Nian Gao (China), Mứt Tết (Vietnam) or Tteokguk (Korea)
- Clean and sweep your house before the New Year
- Give offerings (like **red envelopes** of money) to young family members
- Wear new clothes to signify a fresh start to the New Year

DON'T

- Wash your hair – it washes away good luck!
- Wash clothes on the first two days of the New Year as it is the birthday of the Water God, and is considered an offence to the god
- Do any sweeping on New Year's Day as it is thought to sweep good luck and wealth away
- Speak unlucky words, such as those related to death, sickness or ghosts
- Wear white or black clothes, as the colours are associated with mourning and loss

DECORATIONS & DRESS

Decorations, clothes and gifts are covered in red as the colour symbolizes good luck, happiness and prosperity. Red lanterns are hung up, while red scrolls, marked with well-wishes, are plastered around household doorways. Decorations have gold lettering as gold symbolizes wealth and prosperity. In Vietnam, people wear bright-coloured clothing, not just red.

It is customary to wear formal traditional clothing, such as a **Cheongsam** or **Changshan** (China), **Hanbok** (Korea) or **Áo Dài** (Vietnam) and many still do wear these garments; however, most now prefer to wear modern clothing.

FAMILY REUNION

It is believed if good things come to a family on the first day of the new year, the rest of the year will be full of blessings. In Vietnam, an important Tết ritual is choosing who will be the first person to enter your house in the new year, so someone who is successful and dear to the family is invited to enter first to bring good luck.

People often visit the eldest and most senior members of their family first before visiting other family members and friends. The most important meal of the year is the reunion dinner on New Year's Eve with several generations of your family.

The types of food served for Lunar New Year are highly symbolic. In China, it is a custom to welcome guests with sweet dishes to sweeten the year ahead and to exchange tangerines or oranges as they symbolize wealth and good luck.

People pay respect to ancestors before the new year by making offerings of food, flowers and fruit. For Seollal, a Korean ritual called **charye** is carried out where food is offered to ancestors and then shared by the family.

Sebae is a key part of charye where family members bow to pay respects to their ancestors and elders. Traditionally you'd get down on your knees and bow; however, today many people perform simplified versions.

RED ENVELOPES

Billions of red envelopes filled with money are gifted each year for Lunar New Year. Different cultures have different traditions when it comes to the gifting of red envelopes. Red envelopes are most commonly exchanged from elders to children. For **Tết**, children offer a traditional greeting to their elders before receiving the money packets.

ARTS & CRAFTS

TRAY OF TOGETHERNESS

YOU WILL NEED

- 4 sheets of red A4 paper
  (or any colour of your choice)
- ruler
- scissors
- pens and items to decorate (optional)
- tape

INSTRUCTIONS

1. Fold the paper in half along the width.

2. Unfold and with the paper lengthways, fold the top two corners to the centre, to create a point at the top. Fold the bottom edge of the paper up.

3. Unfold and cut along the crease on the bottom edge to make two rectangles. Then cut along the vertical fold in the centre of the larger rectangle. The other can be discarded. Dont forget to recycle!

4. You will have two squares and two rectangles. Each square will form one container for the Tray of Togetherness.

5. Fold in the sides of one square 3cm from the edge, using your ruler to measure.

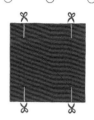

6. Unfold the paper and cut along the lines as marked in white, right.

7. Add patterns or decorations to the containers now.

8. Repeat steps 1 to 7 with the remaining square and the remaining three sheets of red paper to create eight squares.

9. Fold the sides up and tape the flaps together. Place the eight containers on a circular tray and fill with different sweets.

RED LANTERN

YOU WILL NEED

- 1 sheet of red origami paper
- 1 sheet of green origami paper
- 1 sheet of pink origami paper
- pen
- scissors
- pin
- gold tassel
- gold thread or string
- needle

INSTRUCTIONS

1. Trace the flower shape that is on the opposite page onto your paper. Carefully cut it out.

2. Use a pin to poke a hole in the middle of each petal's point and in the centre of the flower.

3. Thread your tassel's string into the hole in the centre. Tie a knot to secure it.

4. Use a needle to thread a piece of gold string (about 60cm long) through each of the petals.

5. Using the thread, gently curve the paper inwards to form a round lantern.

6. Pull the string and points to bring the lantern together and tie a knot on top to secure it. Your lantern is ready to be hung up!

PAPER FIREWORKS

YOU WILL NEED

- red paper
- scissors
- gold pen
- glue
- hole punch
- gold ribbon or string

INSTRUCTIONS

1. Cut the red paper into squares of about 10cm in size. Make as many as you like and set one square aside.

2. Use a gold pen to decorate the squares along the edges.

3. Roll each square into a tube and glue the edges together to form your fireworks.

4. Punch two holes opposite each other on either end of each firework.

5. Cut a 20cm long string for each firework. Thread the string through the holes in each one. Tie a knot at one end.

6. Cut a longer piece of string (about 90cm long). Secure it with a knot to the square you set aside earlier.

7. Use the string in your firework to tie a knot along the longer piece of string.

8. Add a second firework and secure it with a knot.

9. Repeat with the remaining firework, alternating sides. Secure them with a knot.

HANG YOUR PAPER FIREWORKS UP TO KEEP THE NIAN MONSTER AWAY!

SAFETY FIRST
Ask an adult for help when using scissors.

RAT FINGER PUPPET

YOU WILL NEED

- A4 sheet of white paper
- dinner plate
- pens
- scissors
- glue
- coloured pens (optional)

INSTRUCTIONS

1. Use a plate to trace a circle on a sheet of paper and cut it out. Save the leftover paper to make the other parts of the rat.

2. Fold the circle in half and then in half again. Colour and decorate it now, if you want to.

3. Unfold the paper and cut out each quarter circle. Each one will make one rat.

4. Roll each quarter up into a cone. Glue the edges together, gently pressing down to secure them.

5. Use the leftover paper to cut two small circle shapes for the ears, one long thin piece for the tail and two shorter thin strips for whiskers. Colour in the ears.

6. Glue the tail inside the cone and the ears on top of the cone. For the whiskers, cross the two short strips of paper into an "X", shape and glue onto the pointy side of the cone.

7. Use a to pen draw two eyes and a nose.

NOW YOU CAN PUT THE RAT FINGER PUPPETS ON AND PUT ON YOUR OWN NEW YEAR SHOW!

LUCKY RED OX

YOU WILL NEED

- 1 empty toilet paper roll
- red paint
- paintbrush
- white sheet of paper
- black pen
- scissors
- glue stick

SAFETY FIRST
Ask an adult for help when using scissors.

INSTRUCTIONS

1. Paint the toilet roll red – the colour symbolizes good luck.

2. Use a pen to draw an oval on a sheet of white paper. Carefully cut out the oval. Draw two dots for nostrils, and a curved line for a smile beneath.

3. Cut out horns from the white paper.

4. Cut out small white circles and put dots in them for eyes. Once the paint dries, glue the eyes onto the toilet roll.

5. Cut two half-moon shapes at the bottom to form the legs. Draw the feet on both sides of the shapes.

6. Glue on the nose, mouth and horns.

YOUR LUCKY RED OX IS NOW READY TO GO!

TIGER PUPPET

YOU WILL NEED

- piece of orange origami paper
- black pen

INSTRUCTIONS

1. Fold your orange paper in half and then in half again to make a smaller square.

2. Unfold the paper. Take a corner of the sheet and fold it diagonally into the centre of the crease.

3. Fold the remaining corners to the middle.

4. Turn the folded paper over so all the flaps are on the underside of the paper. Fold the corner to the middle again.

5. Fold in half so that the squares (not the triangle shapes) are on the outside.

6. This part is a little tricky. Place your thumb and index (first) finger of both hands each in a square flap. Then, pinch your thumbs and index fingers together.

7. You should have a movable puppet. Now you need to add the details. Draw on some eyes.

8. Holding the puppet closed, draw the nose and black lines going outwards to make the wiskers.

9. Draw black triangles on each of the top corners for the ears. Lastly, draw tiger stripes on all sections.

YOUR TIGER IS READY TO ROAR!

HOPPING RABBIT

YOU WILL NEED

- red paper
- yellow paper
- ruler
- black pen
- scissors
- glue stick

INSTRUCTIONS

1. Draw a rabbit head, paws and feet onto the red paper and cut them out.

2. Draw the eyes, nose and whiskers onto the rabbit face.

3. To make the rabbit's body, cut two 2cm-wide strips of paper, one red, one yellow, from the longest side of your paper.

4. Glue the end of one strip to the other so they make an "L" shape. Then fold one strip over the other, and repeat, back and forth, until it folds like an accordion. Glue the ends together. When it is done, it should be able to stand upright.

5. Glue the feet to the bottom edge of the paper accordion so they stick out from underneath. Then glue the paws to the top edge, also so they stick out.

6. Glue the rabbit head on top of the paws so the paws are sticking out beneath it.

7. Gently stretch out the rabbit's folded body so it can stand up!

NOW YOUR LUCKY RABBIT IS READY TO HOP INTO THE NEW YEAR!

FIRE-BREATHING DRAGON

YOU WILL NEED

- 1 empty toilet roll paper
- 1 sheet of red paper
- googly eyes
- 2 yellow pom-poms around 2½cm wide
- 2 yellow pom-poms around 1½cm wide
- PVA glue
- 3 pieces of tissue paper – red, yellow and orange
- scissors

SAFETY FIRST
Ask an adult for help when using scissors.

INSTRUCTIONS

1. Wrap the toilet roll in red paper and secure it with glue.

2. Glue the googly eyes onto the bigger pom-poms. These are your dragon eyes!

3. Glue each of the dragon eyes to one end of the toilet roll.

4. Glue the smaller pom-poms to the other end of the toilet roll to make your dragon's nostrils.

5. Cut the tissue paper into long strips. Put a drop of glue on the end of each strip, and attach it to the inside of the roll under the dragon's nose. Glue the strips all the way around the roll. Let the glue dry.

6. To make your dragon breathe fire, put your mouth on the end of the paper roll and blow. The flames will flutter in the air!

YOUR FIRE—BREATHING DRAGON IS READY TO WELCOME THE NEW YEAR!

SLITHERING SNAKE

YOU WILL NEED

- 2 sheets of red paper
- 2 sheets of yellow paper
- 1 extra sheet of either colour for the head and tail
- scissors
- glue stick
- googly eyes

INSTRUCTIONS

1. Fold one sheet of paper in half widthways, then fold it twice more so that you have eight sections, as shown here.

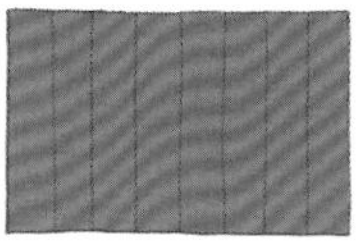

2. Repeat step 1 using the other sheets of paper.

3. Cut along the creases of each sheet of paper so you have eight strips of each colour.

4. Fold a red strip of paper around, until you have a circle, and glue it shut. Loop a yellow strip through the red hoop and glue it shut. Repeat until all the strips of paper have been used.

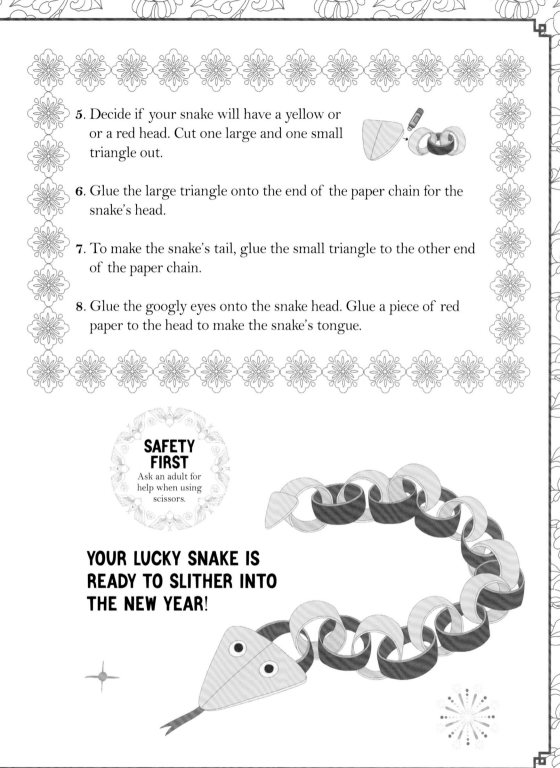

5. Decide if your snake will have a yellow or or a red head. Cut one large and one small triangle out.

6. Glue the large triangle onto the end of the paper chain for the snake's head.

7. To make the snake's tail, glue the small triangle to the other end of the paper chain.

8. Glue the googly eyes onto the snake head. Glue a piece of red paper to the head to make the snake's tongue.

SAFETY FIRST
Ask an adult for help when using scissors.

YOUR LUCKY SNAKE IS READY TO SLITHER INTO THE NEW YEAR!

PAPER ROCKING HORSE

YOU WILL NEED

- yellow card
- small plate
- pen
- black paper
- sheet of red paper

INSTRUCTIONS

1. Use a plate to draw a circle onto the yellow card. Cut the circle out and fold it in half.

2. Draw a semi-circle on the folded line, and cut it out. This is the rocker.

3. Fold the red paper in half and draw two squares on it as shown here.

4. Cut out the two squares, leaving a chair-shape (this is your horse!).

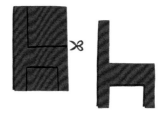

5. Crease diagonally across the top of the 'neck' to make the head of the horse.

6. Open the horse and fold its head forward along the diagonal, either side of the neck.

7. Cut out a black strip the length of the horse's neck. Snip all along one side, without cutting through, to make a mane. Glue the mane inside the neck.

8. Glue the mane inside the neck. Cut out two small red triangles and glue one each side of the horse's head for the ears.

9. Cut four small black rectangles the width of the horse's legs and glue them onto the ends to make the horse's hooves.

10. Cut another black strip to make the tail. Carefully snip vertical lines without cutting through. Glue the tail inside the back of the horse.

11. Cut open the front legs, so that you can stick two legs on each side of the rocker.

12. Use your pen to give your horse a mouth, eyes and nostrils.

13. Unfold the rocker. The horse will stand and rock back and forth when tapped.

FLUFFY LUCKY SHEEP

YOU WILL NEED

- toilet roll
- cotton wool balls
- liquid glue
- black pipe cleaners
- black or white pom-poms (medium and small)
- black sheet of paper
- scissors
- googly eyes

INSTRUCTIONS

1. Glue cotton wool balls all over the entire toilet roll. This will be your sheep's body.

2. Cut two short pieces of black pipe cleaner and glue a small pom-pom to the end of each piece. Glue the legs to the side of the sheep's body.

3. Glue two of the larger pom-poms to the bottom of the sheep's body to create feet.

4. Cut an oval shape out of the black paper for the face and two smaller oval shapes for the ears. Add the googly eyes to the sheep's face.

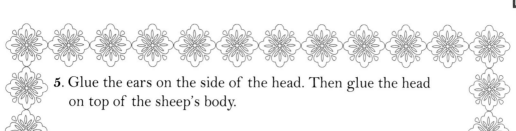

5. Glue the ears on the side of the head. Then glue the head on top of the sheep's body.

6. If you want to add an extra puff of hair on top of the head, pull a little bit of cotton wool from a cotton wool ball and glue it to the top of your sheep's head.

YOUR FLUFFY LUCKY SHEEP IS READY FOR THE NEW YEAR!

SAFETY FIRST
Ask an adult for help when using scissors.

SWINGING MONKEY

YOU WILL NEED

- 3 sheets of red paper
- black pen
- scissors
- a ruler
- 1 sheet of yellow paper
- 1 sheet of white paper
- glue

INSTRUCTIONS

1. Cut an oval out of the red paper to make the monkey's body.

2. Cut a circle out of the red paper. This will be the head.

3. Using the red paper, cut out three rectangular strips for the legs and tail, about 2cm wide and 30cm long.

4. Cut out two smaller rectangle strips, about 2cm by 25cm, from the red paper. These will be the monkey's arms.

5. To make the monkey's arms and legs, fold each strip of red paper back and forth into small squares on top of one another then pull back so that you have concertina shapes.

6. Using the yellow paper, cut out an oval, slightly longer than the monkey's face – this will be the monkey's mouth.

7. From the red paper, cut out two half circles and four small circles. These will be the monkey's ears and its hands and feet.

8. To make the monkey's eyes, cut out two circles from the white paper. Use a black pen to draw the eyes.

9. Glue the hands and feet to the bottom of the arms and legs.

10. Tightly roll another strip of red paper into a circle to make a curly tail. Glue it to the back of the monkey.

11. Glue on the ears, eyes and mouth.

12. Using a pen, draw a line across the mouth to be the monkey's lips, and two dots for the nose.

YOUR MONKEY IS READY TO SWING INTO THE NEW YEAR!

ROOSTER MASK

YOU WILL NEED

- paper plate
- red paint
- paintbrush
- black pen
- scissors
- 1 sheet of red paper

- 1 sheet of yellow paper
- glue
- tape
- elastic thread
- feathers (optional)

INSTRUCTIONS

1. Paint the paper plate red. When dry, draw a large "U" shape and cut it out. This is your mask.

2. Draw and carefully cut out two eyeholes.

3. Draw and cut out a small semi-circle on the red paper. Fold back and forth round in a concertina until you have a small triangle shape. This is your rooster's "crown".

4. Cut a triangle from the yellow paper to use as a beak. Use the red paper to cut a small oval to make a wattle (dangly bit on a rooster's neck).

5. Glue the crown on the top of the paper plate, the beak in the middle under the eyes, and then the wattle under the beak.

6. Tape the elastic thread on either side of the back of the paper plate so you can wear it.

7. Decorate your mask. If you want, you can glue feathers on the edges of the mask!

COCK–A–DOODLE–DOO!
YOUR ROOSTER IS READY TO CROW IN THE NEW YEAR!

CHALLENGE:
Can you use your imagination to create a mask for all twelve animals of the zodiac?

SAFETY FIRST
Ask an adult for help when using scissors.

BARKING DOG

YOU WILL NEED

- 1 sheet of yellow origami paper
- black pen

INSTRUCTIONS

1. Fold the sheet of paper in half diagonally, to create a triangle.

2. Fold one side of the triangle down to meet the base of the triangle. Repeat on the other side.

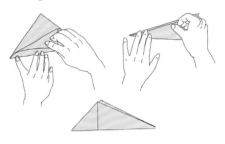

3. Fold back the top two corners that you've just folded.

4. Make a crease by folding down the wider end of your triangle.

5. Open your triangle and push down to reverse the crease back through the inside of the triangle. Open up the two corners you folded in step 4.

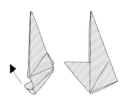

6. Fold the longer triangle across to the right as shown below. Unfold to see the "W" shape. At the bottom of the "W" press down to reverse the creases.

7. Refold the flaps on either side of the body. This is the head.

8. Fold back the point at the front of the dog's head to meet the back of the head. Leaving it folded, bend the point back a little further along. Fold the tip of the triangle back towards the body.

9. Unfold the head. Push the middle crease inwards to create the snout. Do the same fold with the tip of the snout.

10. Unfold the large triangle at the back of your dog's body. Fold the point inwards so that the triangle is flat against the paper.

11. Fold the triangle outwards and fold the body of the dog back together. If you pull the tip of your dog's tail you can make the dog bark.

12. Use a coloured pen to draw eyes, colour in the dog's snout and draw its mouth. Put in a few dots for whiskers.

SAFETY FIRST

Ask an adult for help when using scissors.

DANCING RED PIG

YOU WILL NEED

- 2 paper plates
- red paint
- paint brush
- black pen
- scissors
- googly eyes
- ribbon or string
- glue
- pencil

INSTRUCTIONS

1. Paint two paper plates red and leave to dry.

2. Cut one of the paper plates into a spiral. Start from the outside and work your way to the centre.

3. Cut out a circle in the middle of the second paper plate to make the head.

4. Using the rim of the second plate, cut out two ears, four trotters and a small circle for the snout. Use a black pen to colour the bottom of the trotters and to draw two nostrils on the snout.

5. Cut a small rectangle from the rim of the paper plate. Fold it into thirds, as shown. Glue one side to the pig's snout and the other side to the pig's face.

6. Glue the ears to the pig's head.

7. Glue on googly eyes. Draw on a smile below the pig's snout.

8. Cut a thin strip from the paper plate rim. Wrap it around a pen to make a curly tail. Glue the tail onto the outer rim of the spiral.

9. Glue the head to the top of the spiral body. Glue the trotters on the inside rim of the body and two on the outer rim.

10. Glue the piece of string or ribbon to the back of the head. Tie it to a pencil. You can now make your pig spin and dance around!

YOUR LUCKY RED PIG IS READY TO DANCE INTO THE NEW YEAR!

RECIPES

INGREDIENTS

Some ingredients can be substituted for more commonly found ingredients, but others can only be found in Asian food stores.

SAFETY FIRST

Remember to ask an adult for help when using any sharp equipment, such as knives, or attempting a recipe that requires the use of an oven, hob or electric blender. And have fun creating and sharing these delicious treats!

TRAY OF
TOGETHERNESS

A Tray of Togetherness is an arrangement of sweet offerings used to welcome guests during Lunar New Year. It is thought that sweet foods will bring a sweet life.

Each compartment is used to hold one type of sweet or nut. Items in the tray can be used to signify various well-wishes for the new year and will vary from family to family. A few common examples of items that might be included are:

- Candied coconuts for family unity
- Pistachios for happiness
- Candied ginger for good health
- Sesame balls for good fortune
- Candied winter melon for good health
- Gold chocolate coins for prosperity
- Dried red dates for good luck
- Sweets with red and gold wrappers for blessings
- Dried red watermelon seeds for a joyful life

Similarly for Tết, a tray of sweets, called Mứt Tết, is a key part of the Lunar New Year, and is laid out as an offering to ancestors. This tray of sweets is also served to visiting guests.

CANDIED COCONUT RIBBONS (MỨT DỪA)

This is a fun and festive treat to make during Lunar New Year, especially in Vietnam and something that can be served as part of Mứt Tết (a tray of togetherness). Try making multiple colours to really make the dish stand out!

INGREDIENTS

- 560g strips of coconut in syrup
- 4 tablespoon caster sugar
- ½ tablespoon food colouring

EQUIPMENT

- colander
- bowl
- saucepan
- wooden spoon

SAFETY FIRST
Ask an adult for help when using the hob.

METHOD

1. Strain the coconut strips in a colander and rinse them under running water. Place the coconut strips in a bowl and add the sugar.

2. Leave the mixture for about 30 minutes. When there is a pool of liquid in the bowl mix in ½ tablespoon of food colouring.

3. Add the coconut strips to a non-stick pan. Cook on a medium heat for 15 minutes, and stir the mixture regularly.

4. Turn the heat to low to stop the coconut from burning as it cooks. Stir the coconut strips until there is no liquid left in the pan. This should take around 25 to 30 minutes.

5. Leave the coconut strips in a bowl to cool for 30 minutes before serving.

NEW YEAR CAKE
(NIAN GAO)

One legend says that this sweet treat is offered so that the Kitchen God, who makes an annual report to the Jade Emperor, has a hard time saying any bad things about your family.

INGREDIENTS

- 360ml water
- 400g brown sugar
- 240ml coconut milk
- 1 teaspoon vegetable oil, plus extra for greasing and frying
- 450g glutinous flour
- ½ teaspoon salt

EQUIPMENT

- saucepan
- large bowl
- whisk
- large cake pan
- steamer or heatproof tray and large pan or wok
- knife

STEAMING FOOD

If you don't have a steamer, place a steaming rack into a larger pan or wok and add water. The water should come up to around 2cm below the rack. Bring the water to a boil. Once boiling, place your small pan with the food on top of the rack – the small pan should not touch any of the sides or protrude over the top of the larger pan – and cover the large pan with a lid.

METHOD

1. Add water and sugar to a pan. Bring it to a boil over a medium heat and stir. Once the sugar dissolves remove the pan from the heat and let it cool slightly.

2. Slowly mix the coconut milk and oil into the sugar water.

3. In a large bowl, mix the glutinous flour with the salt.

4. Carefully pour the sugar water mixture into the flour. Whisk as the liquid is added and keep stirring until the batter is smooth with no lumps.

5. Grease a large cake pan and pour the batter into it. Cover the pan with foil.

6. Place the pan in a steamer or a pot if you don't have a steamer. Reduce the heat to medium and steam for 1 hour.

7. Remove the pan from the pot and leave to cool.

8. Slice the new year cake into 1cm thick slices or squares and pan fry with a little oil on both sides until browned before serving.

SAFETY FIRST
Ask an adult for help when using the hob/steamer.

YAKSIK

A traditional Korean dessert, *yaksik* means "medicine food". A key ingredient is honey, which was used as medicine in the past – it is still widely viewed as good for your health in small amounts.

INGREDIENTS

- 500g glutinous rice
- 15 large dried jujubes, rinsed, deseeded (or replace them with 220g dried cranberries)
- 60g raisins
- 2 talespoon pine nuts
- 15 peeled, cooked and quartered chestnuts

EQUIPMENT

- bowl
- sieve
- pot
- rice cooker or a pot
- spatula
- cutting board
- knife
- wooden spoon

SEASONING SAUCE

- 350ml water
- 100ml dark brown sugar
- 50ml runny honey
- 2 tablespoon soy sauce
- 3 tablespoon sesame oil
- 1 teaspoon cinnamon powder
- 1 teaspoon salt

> If you're using a pot to cook rice instead of a rice cooker, cover the pot with a lid. Bring to a boil on a high heat, then reduce the heat to low and cook for 40 to 45 minutes. Remove the pan from the heat and set aside, without lifting the lid, for 10 minutes.

METHOD

1. Rinse the rice in water, until the water runs clear. Soak the rice in a bowl of cold water for at least 6 hours. Strain the water with a sieve.

2. Pour the seasoning sauce ingredients into a pot. On a medium heat, stir to dissolve the sugar, and bring the mixture to a boil. Boil for 2 minutes.

3. Add the glutinous rice to a rice cooker or a pot. Place the sliced jujubes or cranberries, raisins, pine nuts and chestnuts on top of the rice. Pour the sauce on top of the rice and cook on white rice mode. Leave in the rice cooker for an extra 5 minutes after it has finished cooking.

4. Gently stir the rice with a spatula, pour into a greased container and squash the rice down with a spatula. Set aside to cool.

5. Flip the container upside down and set the yaksik onto the cutting board. Cut the yaksik into small rectangles for serving.

SAFETY FIRST
Ask an adult to help when using the hob/ rice cooker/knife.

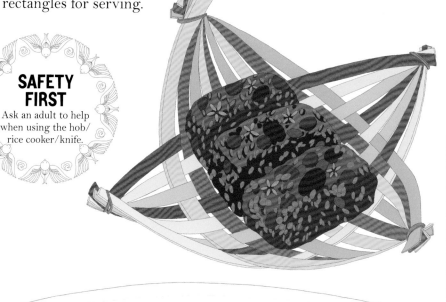

TANGYUAN

This delicious recipe is enjoyed by many families during Lunar New Year. The round shape and the bowls in which they are served is said to represent family unity and togetherness.

INGREDIENTS

TANGYUAN
- 130g glutinous rice flour
- 120ml warm water

TANGYUAN FILLING (OPTIONAL)
- 2 tablespoons peanut butter
- 2 tablespoons sugar

SOUP
- 500ml water
- 100g brown sugar (packed)
- 25g or 4 slices ginger

EQUIPMENT

- mixing bowl
- wooden spoon
- large saucepan
- slotted spoon
- medium saucepan
- serving dish

SAFETY FIRST
Ask an adult for help when using the hob.

METHOD

1. Use a wooden spoon to mix the flour and warm water together in a mixing bowl. Once the dough has formed, knead it into a smooth dough.

2. Divide the dough into twelve pieces. Flatten the dough pieces into discs, so they are around 4cm in diameter.

3. Put a small dab of the peanut butter (about ½ teaspoon) in the the middle of each dough circle. Carefully fold the dough over the peanut butter and roll it into a ball. This is your tangyuan.

4. Fill a large saucepan with water and bring to the boil.

5. Add the tangyuan to the water and boil until they float to the top of the pot. Remove using a slotted spoon. Place into a serving dish.

6. Meanwhile, place 500ml of water in a medium saucepan and add brown sugar and ginger. Bring the water to a boil over a medium heat.

7. Stir until the sugar has dissolved. Boil for 10 minutes until you have a soup.

8. Pour the soup over the tangyuan and serve.

RED BEAN SOUP WITH SAGO

INGREDIENTS

- 125g dried red beans or mung beans, well washed
- 20g sago or tapioca
- 65g caster sugar
- 1.45 litres water

EQUIPMENT

- fine sieve
- pot

SAFETY FIRST
Ask an adult for help when using the hob.

METHOD

1. Rinse the red beans with water. Cover with water and soak overnight.

2. Cover and soak the sago in water for 30 minutes. Drain the water with a fine sieve.

3. Bring a pot of water to a boil and add the sago. Cook for 7 to 10 minutes, until the sago is semi-transparent.

4. Remove the sago from the water with a sieve, then rinse with cold water and set aside in a bowl.

5. Add 1.45 litres of water to a pot and bring to a boil. Add the soaked red beans and bring back to a boil. Turn heat to low and simmer for 1 to 1½ hours until the red beans are soft and have a creamy texture. Add more water if needed.

6. Once cooked, mix in the sugar and sago and enjoy.

TOP TIP:

The tangyuan (glutinous rice balls) from the previous recipe can be added to this soup as well for an extra treat!

WALNUT COOKIES (HUP TOH SOH)

Symbolizing happiness, walnut cookies are a Chinese treat that are perfect to cook and serve as a Lunar New Year's offering to visitors.

INGREDIENTS

- 100g ground walnuts (or broken into small pieces, if preferred)
- 130g plain flour
- 100g caster sugar
- ½ teaspoon salt
- 80g vegetable oil
- 1 medium egg

EQUIPMENT

- bowl
- wire rack

SAFETY FIRST
Ask an adult for help when using the oven.

METHOD

1. Preheat your oven to 180°C or gas mark 4.

2. Except for the eggs, mix all the ingredients together in a bowl, until it has a crumbly texture.

3. Shape the dough into small balls (roughly the size of a walnut). Place on a baking sheet.

4. Beat the egg and brush over the cookies.

5. Bake the cookies for 18 to 20 minutes, until firm and golden. Cool on a wire rack, before eating.

FORTUNE CAKE (FA GAO)

This dessert is sometimes called fortune cake as its Cantonese name – fa gao – sounds like the word for 'wealth' and it is thought to bring wealth in the New Year! The top of this cake should crack and look like a smile when cooked properly.

INGREDIENTS

- 3 tablespoons baking powder
- vegetable oil (for greasing)
- 200g plain flour
- 80g sugar
- 200ml water

EQUIPMENT

- 4 glass or ceramic moulds
- saucepan
- sieve
- steamer or large pan
- steaming rack
- wooden spoon

STEAMING FOOD

If you don't have a steamer, place a steaming rack into a larger pan or wok and add water. The water should come up to around 2cm below the rack. Bring the water to a boil. Once boiling, place your small pan with the food on top of the rack – the small pan should not touch any of the sides or protrude over the top of the larger pan – and cover the large pan with a lid.

SAFETY FIRST

Ask an adult for help when using the hob/steamer.

METHOD

1. Grease four small glass or ceramic moulds and set aside.

2. Place the sugar and water into a saucepan over medium heat. Stir until the sugar has dissolved and pour into a large bowl.

3. Sieve in the flour and baking powder and mix together until the batter is smooth.

4. Pour the mixture into the moulds and steam on a high heat for 20 minutes until the cakes have risen and have cooked through.

RICE CAKE SOUP (TTEOKGUK)

This is a traditional Korean dish eaten during the Lunar New Year. The round rice cakes symbolize coins for prosperity.

INGREDIENTS

- 1.7 litres water
- 225g flank skirt steak or brisket
- 3 garlic cloves
- 3 spring onions
- 2 teaspoons vegetable oil
- 2 large eggs
- 450g Korean rice cakes
- 1 tablespoon fish sauce
- 1 teaspoon sesame oil
- ½ teaspoon ground black pepper
- salt
- 2-3 sheets Korean roasted seaweed

EQUIPMENT

- large pot
- frying pan
- knife

SAFETY FIRST

Ask an adult for help when using the hob/knife.

METHOD

1. Ask an adult to help you chop your meat into 2cm pieces and finely slice your garlic cloves.

2. Add water to a pot and bring to a boil. Add the meat and the garlic. Cook on a high heat for 5 minutes. Simmer on a medium heat for 30 minutes.

3. Meanwhile, heat the vegetable oil in a small frying pan over a low heat.

4. Separate the egg whites and yolks. Ask an adult to fry both sides of the yolks for 1 to 2 minutes until cooked. Ask an adult to slice them into thin strips.

5. Add the rice cakes to the soup and cover the pan. Simmer for 8 minutes until the cakes have softened and float to the surface.

6. Ask an adult to slice the spring onions and add them to the soup. Add the fish sauce, salt, sesame oil and pepper.

7. Slowly pour the egg whites into the soup, stirring as you add them. Cook for another 30 seconds.

8. Remove the pot from the heat. Cut the seaweed into slices. Ladle the soup into bowls and garnish with the egg and seaweed strips.

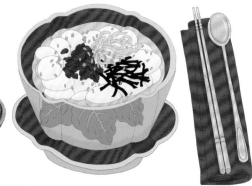

TURNIP CAKE (LO BAK GOH)

This dish can be enjoyed year-round, but it is often prepared during Lunar New Year as the turnip or white radish symbolizes fortune.

INGREDIENTS

- 1.3kg Chinese turnip / daikon / mooli radish
- 225g rice flour
- 120ml water
- 65g sausage, diced (Chinese sausage optional)
- 1½ teaspoon salt
- 2 tablespoons vegetable oil, plus extra for frying
- 1 teaspoon sesame oil
- 2 garlic cloves
- 2 teaspoons chicken bouillon powder
- ½ teaspoon white pepper
- 4 spring onions

EQUIPMENT

- grater
- large pot
- frying pan
- knife
- cake tin
- steamer or large pot
- steaming rack
- wooden spoon

If you don't have a steamer, place the covered pan on a rack inside a larger pot. The smaller pan shouldn't touch the sides or poke over the top of the larger pot. Fill the larger pot with water – it should come up to around 2cm below the rack. Bring the water to a boil. Place the cake tin on top of the rack and cover the pan with a lid.

METHOD

1. Ask an adult to coarsely grate the Chinese turnip or radish. Place into a large pot and add water. Cover the pan and cook for 5 to 10 minutes over a medium heat, until wilted.

2. Heat the vegetable oil in a frying pan on a medium heat. Finely chop the garlic and spring onions and dice the sausage, and add to the pan. Cook for about 3 to 5 minutes, then add to the Chinese turnip or radish.

3. Add the flour and the rest of the ingredients into the wilted turnip or radish and mix well.

4. Pour the mixture into a cake tin, cover with foil and steam for 1 hour on a medium heat.

5. Once cool, cut the cake into small rectangles. Fry in a small amount of oil until brown on both sides.

SAFETY FIRST
Ask an adult for help when using the hob/steamer/grater.

LONGEVITY NOODLES

Long noodles symbolize a long life and are popular at New Year!

INGREDIENTS

- 225g of long wheat noodles
- 3 garlic cloves
- 25g ginger
- 2 tablespoons soy sauce
- 4 spring onions
- 1½ tablespoon sesame oil
- 1 teaspoon sesame seeds

EQUIPMENT

- large pot
- serving bowl
- knife

SAFETY FIRST

Ask an adult for help when using the hob.

METHOD

1. Bring a pot of water to a boil. Add the noodles and cook for 4 to 5 minutes. Drain and rinse the noodles with cold water until cool, and set aside.

2. Finely chop the garlic and ginger before mixing with sesame oil and soy sauce. Mix the ingredients together and pour over the noodles.

3. Slice the spring onions. Garnish the noodles with the sliced spring onions and sesame seeds.

DUMPLINGS (JIAOZI)

A Chinese New Year staple, dumplings symbolize wealth because their shape resembles a Chinese **sycee**, gold ingots that used to be used as currency in China.

INGREDIENTS

- 450g pork mince
- 170g napa cabbage minced (other cabbage can be substituted)
- 2 spring onions
- 1 large egg, beaten
- 3 tablespoons soy sauce
- 2 teaspoons sesame oil
- 1 teaspoon rice wine
- 20g ginger
- 1 teaspoon ground white pepper
- 50 pre-made dumpling wrappers

EQUIPMENT

- large bowl
- tray
- large pot
- slotted spoon
- serving dish

SAFETY FIRST

Ask an adult for help when using the hob/greater.

METHOD

1. To make the filling, chop the cabbage and the spring onions into slices and grate the ginger. Mix all the ingredients, except the dumpling wrappers, together in a large bowl.

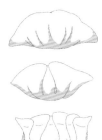

2. Place a tablespoon of filling in the centre of a dumpling wrapper. Wet the edges of the wrapper with water. Fold the edges over and pinch together, forming pleats, to make a dumpling – any number of pleats will work.

3. Place the dumplings onto a flour-lined tray. The flour will stop the dumplings from sticking to the tray.

4. Bring a large pot of water to the boil and carefully add the dumplings in batches, and cook for 5 to 6 minutes. Be careful not to add too many at a time! Remove with a slotted spoon and place onto a serving dish when cooked.

MY LUNAR NEW YEAR

USE THE PAGES AT THE BACK OF THIS BOOK
TO NOTE DOWN HOW YOU CELEBRATED LUNAR NEW YEAR

MY LUNAR NEW YEAR
JOURNAL

Use this space to keep a record of any special Lunar New Year memories.

DATE: _____

I SPENT LUNAR NEW YEAR WITH:

_____

MY FAVOURITE PART OF LUNAR NEW YEAR WAS:

_____

_____

_____

_____

_____

DRAW A PICTURE OF YOUR
LUNAR NEW YEAR CELEBRATION BELOW!

MY GOALS FOR
THE COMING YEAR

You can use this page to write down three things you would like to do in the next year.

Perhaps you are going to help out around the house more or maybe you are going to pick up litter in the park or at the beach. Perhaps you might try and learn a new skill or sport. Remember to check on this list over the coming year to make sure you are keeping up with your goals.

NOTES

GLOSSARY

Áo dài – a traditional Vietnamese women's dress made up of a long-sleeved tunic with ankle-length panels at the sides, worn over trousers.

Changshan – a long jacket or robe, traditionally worn by Chinese men.

Charye – an important Korean ritual performed during Seollal, where food is offered to one's ancestors and is later shared by the family.

Cheongsam – a traditional Chinese dress for women, a cheongsam has a slit in the skirt with a mandarin collar.

Chūn Jié – a Chinese holiday that celebrates the New Year. It is also known as the Spring Festival.

Gregorian calendar – a calendar that uses the Sun's cycle to keep track of the time. The year is divided into twelve months and has 365 days. It is the most commonly used calendar in the world.

Hanbok – a traditional Korean dress worn by women, hanboks are usually very vibrant and colourful.

Hemisphere – one half of a sphere or a ball. A hemisphere is used to describe one half of the Earth as if you draw a circle around the Earth it divides the planet into two halves – the northern and southern hemispheres or the eastern and western hemispheres.

Lunisolar calendar – a calendar that uses the cycles of the Sun and Moon to keep track of the passing of time and the changing seasons.

Migration – an annual movement of animals or people at a specific time of the year.

Moon – a planetary satellite, which means a planet or moon that orbits a planet. The Moon is the Earth's only natural satellite.

Orbit – the journey of a planetary body around another. The Earth travels around the Sun.

Red envelopes – a gift given in East and Southeast Asian cultures to commemorate special occasions, usually filled with money.

Sebae – a part of the ritual of charye, in which family members bow to pay their respects to their elders and ancestors.

Seollal – a festival celebrated in Korea, celebrating the New Year.

Solstice – a solstice occurs when either of the Earth's magnetic poles reaches its furthest tilt away from the Sun. A solstice occurs twice in a year, once in the summer and again in the winter.

Sun – the Sun is the closest star to Earth. The Sun's heat and light supports life on Earth, sunlight helps plants to grow, it produces oxygen and food for people to eat. The Sun's heat also keeps the Earth warm – without it our planet would freeze.

Sycee – a type of currency that was used in China in the past.

Tết Nguyên Đán – a Vietnamese festival commemorating the New Year.

ABOUT THE AUTHOR

KEVIN TSANG was born in Copenhagen, Denmark, grew up in Atlanta, Georgia, USA, previously lived in Hong Kong, and is currently based in London with his wife and their young daughters. Kevin's parents are from Hong Kong. He always enjoyed celebrating Lunar New Year as a child, and now celebrates with his own children. Kevin graduated from the University of Georgia and also studied abroad at the Chinese University of Hong Kong, which is where he met his wife, Katie.

Together, they write the *SAM WU IS NOT AFRAID* and *SPACE BLASTERS* series, as well as the bestselling *DRAGON REALM* series. When Kevin isn't writing children's fiction, he enjoys cooking on the grill and spending time with his family.

ABOUT THE ILLUSTRATOR

LINH NGUYEN grew up in Hanoi, Vietnam. She celebrates Lunar New Year every year as an important family tradition. She now shares the joy of Tết with her Scottish husband, Michael, while building a cross-cultural family of her own. After graduating from the University of the West of England, Bristol with a master's degree in animation, Linh found herself fascinated by visual storytelling and cultural heritage projects. Since then, Linh has dedicated herself to a full-time illustration career with a style rich in vibrant tones. Her artworks can be found under the name 'Folktales by Linh' (www.folktalesbylinh.com). She wishes to contribute to the enrichment of the modern world's narratives – facilitating the telling of stories as they tell themselves.